Congressional Research Service
Informing the legislative debate since 1914

SBA Assistance to Small Business Startups: Client Experiences and Program Impact

Robert Jay Dilger
Senior Specialist in American National Government

February 26, 2014

Congressional Research Service

7-5700

www.crs.gov

R43083

Summary

The Small Business Administration (SBA) administers several programs to support small businesses, including loan guaranty and venture capital programs to enhance small business access to capital; contracting programs to increase small business opportunities in federal contracting; direct loan programs for businesses, homeowners, and renters to assist their recovery from natural disasters; and small business management and technical assistance training programs to assist business formation and expansion.

Congressional interest in these programs, and the SBA's assistance provided to small business startups in particular (defined as new businesses that meet the SBA's criteria as small), has increased in recent years, primarily because these programs are viewed by many as a means to stimulate economic activity, create jobs, and assist in the national economic recovery.

Economists generally do not view job creation as a justification for providing federal assistance to small businesses. They argue that in the long term such assistance will likely reallocate jobs within the economy, not increase them. In their view, jobs arise primarily from the size of the labor force, which depends largely on population, demographics, and factors that affect the choice of home versus market production (e.g., the entry of women in the workforce). However, economic theory does suggest that increased federal spending on small business assistance programs may result in additional jobs in the short term.

Congressional interest in assistance to business startups is derived primarily from economic research suggesting that startups play a very important role in job creation. That research suggests that business startups create many new jobs, but have a more limited effect on net job creation over time because fewer than half of all startups remain in business after five years. However, that research also suggests that the influence of small business startups on net job creation varies by firm size. Startups with fewer than 20 employees tend to have a negligible effect on net job creation over time whereas startups with 20-499 employees tend to have a positive employment effect, as do surviving younger businesses of all sizes (in operation for one year to five years).

This report examines small business startups' experiences with the SBA's management and technical assistance training programs, focusing on Small Business Development Centers (SBDCs), Women Business Centers (WBCs), and SCORE (Service Corps of Retired Executives); the 7(a), 504/CDC, and Microloan lending programs; and the Small Business Investment Company (SBIC) venture capital program. Although data collected by the SBA concerning these programs' impact on economic activity and job creation are somewhat limited and subject to methodological challenges concerning their validity as reliable performance measures, most small business owners who have participated in these programs report in surveys sponsored by the SBA that the programs were useful. Given the data limitations, however, it is difficult to determine the cost effectiveness of these programs.

Two recent SBA initiatives designed to assist small business startups are also discussed: the SBA's growth accelerators initiative, which targets entrepreneurs looking to "start and scale their business" helping them access "seed capital, mentors, and networking opportunities for customers and partners," and the SBA's $1 billion early stage debenture SBIC initiative.

Contents

Tables

Contacts

The SBA's Missions

The Small Business Administration (SBA) administers several programs to support small businesses, including the 7(a) and 504/CDC loan guaranty programs and Microloan lending program to enhance small business access to capital; the Small Business Investment Company (SBIC) program to enhance small business access to venture capital; contracting programs to increase small business opportunities in federal contracting; direct loan programs for businesses, homeowners, and renters to assist their recovery from natural disasters; and small business management and technical assistance training programs to assist business formation and expansion.[1] Congressional interest in these programs, and the SBA's assistance to small business startups in particular (defined as new businesses that meet the SBA's criteria as small), has increased in recent years, primarily because these programs are viewed by many as a means to stimulate economic activity, create jobs, and assist in the national economic recovery.

The Small Business Act specifies four missions for the SBA:

> It is the declared policy of the Congress that the Government should aid, counsel, assist, and protect, insofar as is possible, the interests of small-business concerns in order to preserve free competitive enterprise, to insure that a fair proportion of the total purchases and contracts or subcontracts for property and services for the Government (including but not limited to contracts or subcontracts for maintenance, repair, and construction) be placed with small-business enterprises, to insure that a fair proportion of the total sales of Government property be made to such enterprises, and to maintain and strengthen the overall economy of the Nation.[2]

As part of its mission to maintain and strengthen the overall economy of the nation, the SBA has always been interested in promoting job creation and job retention.[3] For example, the SBA currently gathers data from its clients concerning the number of jobs either created or retained as a result of the assistance they receive from the SBA. The SBA refers to these self-reported data as the number of "jobs supported." The SBA also regularly sponsors research on the role of small businesses in job creation and retention, and considers that research when designing its programs.

Economists generally do not view job creation as a justification for providing federal assistance to small businesses. They argue that in the long term such assistance will likely reallocate jobs within the economy, not increase them. In their view, jobs arise primarily from the size of the

---

[1] U.S. Small Business Administration, "Fiscal Year 2014 Congressional Budget Justification and FY2012 Annual Performance Report," p. 1. For further analysis of the SBA's loan guaranty programs see CRS Report R41146, *Small Business Administration 7(a) Loan Guaranty Program*, by Robert Jay Dilger; and CRS Report R41184, *Small Business Administration 504/CDC Loan Guaranty Program*, by Robert Jay Dilger. For further analysis of the SBA's Small Business Investment Company program see CRS Report R41456, *SBA Small Business Investment Company Program*, by Robert Jay Dilger. For further analysis of the New Markets Venture Capital program see CRS Report R42565, *SBA New Markets Venture Capital Program*, by Robert Jay Dilger. For further analysis of the SBA's disaster loan programs see CRS Report R41309, *The SBA Disaster Loan Program: Overview and Possible Issues for Congress*, by Bruce R. Lindsay. For further analysis of the SBA's contracting programs see CRS Report R40744, *The "8(a) Program" for Small Businesses Owned and Controlled by the Socially and Economically Disadvantaged: Legal Requirements and Issues*, by Kate M. Manuel, and CRS Report R41268, *Small Business Administration HUBZone Program*, by Robert Jay Dilger.

[2] 15 U.S.C. §631; P.L. 83-163, the Small Business Act of 1953 (as amended).

[3] U.S. Senate, Select Committee on Small Business, Citation of Statement by Wendell B. Barnes, SBA Administrator, *Annual Report*, 83rd Cong., 2nd sess., March 25, 1954, H.Rept. 83-1092 (Washington: GPO, 1954), p. 60.

labor force, which depends largely on population, demographics, and factors that affect the choice of home versus market production (e.g., the entry of women in the workforce). However, economic research does suggest that increased federal spending on small business assistance programs may result in additional jobs in the short term.[4]

Small Business Startups and Job Creation

The SBA's interest, and congressional interest, in providing assistance to small business startups is derived primarily from economic research indicating that startups play an important role in job creation.[5] That research suggests that startups create many, and in some years almost all, net jobs in the national economy. For example, from March 2009 to March 2010 (the latest data available), 533,945 new employer firms were formed (startups) in the United States, about 9.3% of all employer firms (5,734,538).[6] Startups created 2,697,105 jobs during that time frame while non-startups lost 5,232,247 jobs (non-startups created 11,132,049 new jobs, but lost 16,364,296 jobs through either firm contractions or deaths).[7]

Although there is a consensus that startups have an important role in job creation and retention, economic research suggests that startups have a more limited effect on net job creation over time because fewer than half of all startups are still in business after five years. That research also suggests that the influence of startups on net job creation varies by firm size. Startups with fewer than 20 employees tend to have a negligible effect on net job creation over time whereas startups with 20-499 employees tend to have a positive employment effect, as do surviving younger businesses of all sizes (in operation for one year to five years).[8]

---

[4] For further information concerning economic research and small business assistance see CRS Report R41392, *Small Business and the Expiration of the 2001 Tax Rate Reductions: Economic Issues*, by Jane G. Gravelle and Sean Lowry; CRS Report RL32254, *Small Business Tax Benefits: Current Law and Main Arguments For and Against Them*, by Gary Guenther; and CRS Report R41523, *Small Business Administration and Job Creation*, by Robert Jay Dilger. For an economic argument to repeal the SBA see Veronique de Rugy, *Why the Small Business Administration's Loan Programs Should Be Abolished*, American Enterprise Institute for Public Policy Research, AEI Working Paper #126, April 13, 2006, at http://www.aei.org/files/2006/04/13/20060414_wp126.pdf.

[5] Charles Brown, James Hamilton, and James Medoff, *Employers Large and Small* (Cambridge: Harvard University Press, 1990); Zoltan Acs, William Parsons, and Spencer Tracy, "High-Impact Firms: Gazelles Revisited," U.S. Small Business Administration, Office of Advocacy, June 2008, at http://archive.sba.gov/advo/research/rs328tot.pdf; Dane Stangler and Robert E. Litan, "Where Will The Jobs Come From?" Kaufman Foundation Research Series: Firm Formation and Economic Growth, November 2009, at http://www kauffman.org/uploadedfiles/where_will_the_jobs_come_from.pdf; and Dane Stangler and Paul Kedrosky, "Neutralism and Entrepreneurship: The Structural Dynamics of Startups, Young Firms, and Job Creation," Kaufman Foundation Research Series: Firm Formation and Economic Growth, September 2010, at http://www.kauffman.org/uploadedfiles/firm-formation-neutralism.pdf.

[6] U.S. Small Business Administration, "Statistics of U.S. Businesses, U.S. Dynamic Data, U.S. Data: Employer Firm Births and Deaths by Employment Size of Firm, 1989-2010," at http://www.sba.gov/advocacy/849/12162; and U.S. Bureau of the Census, "Statistics of U.S. Businesses: Latest SUSB Annual Data, 2010, U.S. & States Totals," October 2012, at http://www.census.gov/econ/susb/.

[7] U.S. Small Business Administration, "Statistics of U.S. Businesses, U.S. Dynamic Data, U.S. Data: Employer Firm Births and Deaths by Employment Size of Firm, 1989-2010," at http://www.sba.gov/advocacy/849/12162.

[8] Zoltan Acs, William Parsons, and Spencer Tracy, "High-Impact Firms: Gazelles Revisited," U.S. Small Business Administration, Office of Advocacy, June 2008, at http://archive.sba.gov/advo/research/rs328tot.pdf; Dane Stangler and Robert E. Litan, "Where Will The Jobs Come From?" Kaufman Foundation Research Series: Firm Formation and Economic Growth, November 2009, at http://www.kauffman.org/uploadedFiles/where_will_the_jobs_come_from.pdf; John Haltiwanger, Ron S. Jarmin, and Javier Miranda, "Who Creates Jobs? Small vs. Large vs. Young," Cambridge, (continued...)

Given the relatively high rate of firm deaths among startups, providing SBA assistance to startups, especially in the form of a SBA guaranteed loan or venture capital investment, is generally viewed as a relatively "high risk-high reward" endeavor, with advocates focusing on the possibility of job creation and opponents focusing on the risk of default. For example, opponents point to the SBA's experiences with its SBIC Participating Securities program as an example of the risk in providing venture capital to startups. The SBIC Participating Securities program was established in 1994, with congressional authorization, to encourage the formation of participating securities SBICs that would make equity investments in startup and early stage small businesses.[9] The SBA created the program to fill a perceived investment gap created by the SBIC debenture program's focus on investments in mid- and later-stage small businesses.[10] The SBA stopped issuing new commitments for participation securities on October 1, 2004, following relatively major losses (exceeding $2.7 billion in losses on investments of just over $6.0 billion) in the program following the burst of the "technology stock market bubble" from 2000 to 2002.[11] The SBA's action began a process to end the program, which continues today.

Report Overview

This report examines startups' experiences with the SBA's management and technical assistance training programs, focusing on Small Business Development Centers (SBDCs), Women Business Centers (WBCs), and SCORE (Service Corps of Retired Executives); the 7(a), 504/CDC, and Microloan lending programs; and the SBIC venture capital program. Two recent SBA initiatives designed to assist startups are also discussed: the SBA's growth accelerators initiative and the SBA's $1 billion early stage debenture SBIC initiative.

With some notable exceptions, such as the Microloan lending program, the SBA's $1 billion early stage debenture SBIC initiative, and SBA's growth accelerators initiative, these programs are designed to assist small businesses at all developmental stages, as opposed to targeting startups for special attention. Nonetheless, all of these programs provide assistance to startups, and report both outcome data (e.g., the number of small businesses receiving training and the number and amount of loans and venture capital provided) and performance data (e.g., the usefulness of the training and the number of jobs supported by the loan) based on the age of the business. As a result, the experiences of startups can be compared with the experiences of older firms both

---

(...continued)

MA: National Bureau of Economic Research, Working Paper 16300, August 2010, at http://www.nber.org/papers/w16300; and Ian Hathaway, "Small Business and Job Creation: The Unconventional Wisdom," *Bloomberg Government*, October 31, 2011.

[9] P.L. 102-366, the Small Business Credit and Business Opportunity Enhancement Act of 1992 (Title IV, the Small Business Equity Enhancement Act of 1992). For further information and analysis of the SBIC program see CRS Report R41456, *SBA Small Business Investment Company Program*, by Robert Jay Dilger.

[10] Debenture SBICs are required to pay interest and SBA annual charges semi-annually on their debentures through maturity. As a result, although debenture SBICs make a broad range of equity investments, they generally invest in later-stage and mezzanine companies which demonstrate an ability to make early and regular payments on the investment. Participating securities SBICs were not required to make these semi-annual payments to encourage investments in firms, such as startups, which had not yet established an ability to make early and regular payments on the investment.

[11] U.S. Congress, House Committee on Small Business, *Proposed Legislative Remedy for the Participating Securities Program*, 109th Cong., 1st sess., July 27, 2005, Serial No. 109-27 (Washington: GPO, 2005), p. 3; and U.S. Small Business Administration, Office of Inspector General, "The SBIC Program: At Significant Risk For Losses," May 24, 2004, at http://www.sba.gov/office-of-inspector-general/7501/12410.

within and across the SBA's programs. For example, as will be shown, the SBA programs that specifically target startups for special attention provide a relatively larger share of its assistance to startups than other SBA programs.

Although the data collected by the SBA concerning these programs' impact on economic activity and job creation are somewhat limited and subject to methodological challenges concerning their validity as reliable performance measures, most small business owners who have participated in these programs report in surveys sponsored by the SBA that the programs were useful. Given the data limitations, however, it is difficult to determine the cost effectiveness of these programs.

SBA Management and Technical Assistance Training Programs

The SBA has provided management and technical assistance training "to small-business concerns, by advising and counseling on matters in connection with government procurement and on policies, principles and practices of good management" since it began operations in 1953.[12] Initially, the SBA provided its own management and technical assistance training programs. Over time, the SBA has relied increasingly on third parties to provide that training. The SBA reports that more than 1 million aspiring entrepreneurs and small business owners receive training from an SBA-supported resource partner each year.[13]

The SBA has argued that its support of management and technical assistance training for small businesses has contributed "to the long-term success of these businesses and their ability to grow and create jobs."[14] It currently provides financial support to about "14,000 resource partners," including 63 lead SBDCs and more than 900 SBDC local outreach locations, 108 WBCs, and 354 chapters of the mentoring program, SCORE.[15]

The SBDC, WBC, and SCORE programs are the SBA's three largest management and technical assistance training programs.[16] These programs provide training assistance to small businesses as all stages of development, and do not target their assistance exclusively at startups.

All three of these programs provide assistance to small businesses, as defined by the SBA's size standards and regulations.[17] However, there are some differences in the small businesses that tend

---

[12] U.S. Congress, Senate Committee on Banking and Currency, *Extension of the Small Business Act of 1953*, report to accompany S. 2127, 84th Cong., 1st sess., July 22, 1955, S.Rept. 84-1350 (Washington: GPO, 1955), p. 17.

[13] U.S. Small Business Administration, "FY2014 Congressional Budget Justification and FY2012 Annual Performance Report," p. 47, at http://www.sba.gov/sites/default/files/files/1-FY%202014%20CBJ%20FY%202012%20APR.PDF.

[14] U.S. Small Business Administration, "Fiscal Year 2011 Congressional Budget Justification and FY2009 Annual Performance Report," p. 4, at http://www.sba.gov/sites/default/files/files/ FY%202013%20CBJ%20FY%202011%20APR.pdf.

[15] U.S. Small Business Administration, "FY2014 Congressional Budget Justification and FY2012 Annual Performance Report," p. 47, at http://www.sba.gov/sites/default/files/files/1-FY%202014%20CBJ%20FY%202012%20APR.PDF; and U.S. Small Business Administration, "Women's Business Centers Directory," at http://www.sba.gov/about-offices-content/1/2895/resources/13729.

[16] For further information and analysis concerning the SBA's management and technical assistance training programs, see CRS Report R41352, *Small Business Management and Technical Assistance Training Programs*, by Robert Jay Dilger.

---

to seek their services. For example, SBDC clients tend to be somewhat larger, both in terms of annual revenue and employment, than SCORE and WBC clients.[18] Also, as one might expect given its mission, WBCs clients are more likely to be female than SBDC and SCORE clients.[19]

SBDCs, WBCs, and SCORE

SBDCs are "hosted by leading universities, colleges, and state economic development agencies" to deliver management and technical assistance training "to small businesses and nascent entrepreneurs (pre-venture) in order to promote growth, expansion, innovation, increased productivity and management improvement."[20] These services are delivered, in most instances, on a non-fee, one-on-one confidential counseling basis and are administered by 63 lead service centers, with at least one located in each state (four in Texas and six in California), the District of Columbia, Puerto Rico, the Virgin Islands, Guam, and American Samoa.[21] These lead centers manage more than 900 service centers located throughout the United States and the territories.[22] In FY2012, SBDCs provided management and technical assistance training services to 332,421 clients, including about 62,000 long-term clients (at least five hours of counseling contact and preparation time).[23]

WBCs are private, nonprofit organizations which provide financial, management, and marketing assistance to small businesses, including startup businesses, owned and controlled by women. Since its inception, the program has targeted the needs of socially and economically disadvantaged women.[24] In FY2012, WBCs provided management and technical assistance training services to 136,951 clients.[25]

(...continued)

[17] For further information and analysis concerning the SBA's size standards see CRS Report R40860, *Small Business Size Standards: A Historical Analysis of Contemporary Issues*, by Robert Jay Dilger.

[18] In 2012, SBDC clients had average revenue of $762,962 and, on average, 10.05 employees; SCORE clients had average revenue of $465,828 and, on average, 5.56 employees; and WBC clients had average revenue of $192,734 and, on average, 4.67 employees. See U.S. Small Business Administration, Office of Entrepreneurial Development, "Impact Study of Entrepreneurial Dynamics: Office of Entrepreneurial Development Resource Partners' Face-to-Face Counseling," September 2013, p. 26, at http://www.sba.gov/sites/default/files/files/ OED_ImpactReport_09302013_Final.pdf.

[19] In 2012, 82% of the businesses served by WBCs were owned by a female compared to 47% of the businesses served by SBDCs and 47% of the businesses served by SCORE. See U.S. Small Business Administration, Office of Entrepreneurial Development, "Impact Study of Entrepreneurial Dynamics: Office of Entrepreneurial Development Resource Partners' Face-to-Face Counseling," September 2013, p. 17, at http://www.sba.gov/sites/default/files/files/ OED_ImpactReport_09302013_Final.pdf.

[20] U.S. Small Business Administration, "Small Business Development Center Fy/Cy 2011 Program Announcement for Renewal of the Cooperative Agreement for Current Recipient Organizations," p. 3, at http://archive.sba.gov/idc/groups/ public/documents/sba_program_office/sbdc_2011_prgm_announce.pdf.

[21] Ibid.

[22] Association of Small Business Development Centers, "Welcome," Burke, Virginia, at http://www.asbdc-us.org/; and U.S. Small Business Administration, "FY2014 Congressional Budget Justification and FY2012 Annual Performance Report," p. 48, at http://www.sba.gov/sites/default/files/files/1-FY%202014%20CBJ%20FY%202012%20APR.PDF.

[23] Ibid.

[24] Ibid.; and U.S. Congress, House Committee on Small Business, *Review of Women's Business Center Program*, 106th Cong., February 11, 1999, Serial No. 106-2 (Washington: GPO, 1999), p. 4.

[25] U.S. Small Business Administration, "FY2014 Congressional Budget Justification and FY2012 Annual Performance Report," p. 49, at http://www.sba.gov/sites/default/files/files/1-FY%202014%20CBJ%20FY%202012%20APR.PDF.

SCORE is a national volunteer organization which provides management and technical assistance training to small business owners and prospective owners.[26] In FY2012, SCORE's volunteer network of more than 13,000 business professionals provided management and technical assistance training services to 458,773 clients.[27]

Program Performance

In addition to compiling program output data, such as the number of clients served, since 2003 the SBA's Office of Entrepreneurial Development has commissioned an annual "multi-year time series study to assess the impact of the programs it offers to small businesses."[28] The survey asks questions about several aspects of the client's experiences with these programs, including the impact of the programs on their staffing decisions and management practices. The survey is sent each year to a stratified random sample of clients participating in the SBDC, WBC, and SCORE programs. The survey responses are published by the SBA and include the responses of nascent clients (individuals who have taken one or more steps to start a business), startup clients (individuals who have been in business one year or less), and in-business clients (individuals who have been in business more than one year and their business was classified as small by the SBA).

The 2012 survey was released in February 2013. There were 8,263 SBDC client respondents (19% response rate), 7,217 SCORE client respondents (16% response rate), and 340 WBC client respondents (15% response rate).

The survey data reported in **Table 1** through **Table 6** indicate that (1) these programs assisted small businesses at all stages of development, (2) most of the respondents reported that the assistance they received was useful, and (3) most of the respondents reported that the assistance they received resulted in them changing their management practices or strategies. However, relatively few of the respondents reported that the assistance they received resulted in them hiring new staff, retaining staff, or increasing their profit margin.

A statistical analysis of the survey data conducted by the survey's authors suggested that clients receiving three or more hours of counseling, female clients, startups, and clients owning relatively large small businesses were more likely, at a statistically significant level, than clients receiving less than three hours of counseling, male clients, non-startups, and clients owning relatively smaller businesses to report positive results concerning the financial impact of the assistance they received.[29]

---

[26] U.S. Congress, Senate Select Committee on Small Business and House Select Committee on Small Business, *1966 Federal Handbook for Small Business: A Survey of Small Business Programs in the Federal Government Agencies*, committee print, 89th Cong., 3rd sess., January 31, 1966 (Washington: GPO, 1966), p. 5; and U.S. Congress, House Committee on Small Business, Subcommittee on Rural Development, Entrepreneurship, and Trade, *Subcommittee Hearing on Legislative Initiatives to Modernize SBA's Entrepreneurial Development Programs*, 111th Cong., 1st sess., April 2, 2009 (Washington: GPO, 2009), p. 6.

[27] U.S. Small Business Administration, "FY2014 Congressional Budget Justification and FY2012 Annual Performance Report," p. 50, at http://www.sba.gov/sites/default/files/files/1-FY%202014%20CBJ%20FY%202012%20APR.PDF.

[28] U.S. Small Business Administration, Office of Entrepreneurial Development, "Impact Study of Entrepreneurial Development Resources," September 10, 2009, p. 2, at http://archive.sba.gov/idc/groups/public/documents/sba_program_office/ed_finalreport_2009.pdf.

[29] U.S. Small Business Administration, Office of Entrepreneurial Development, "Impact Study of Entrepreneurial Dynamics: Office of Entrepreneurial Development Resource Partners' Face-to-Face Counseling," September 2012, p. 70, at http://www.sba.gov/sites/default/files/files/SBA_Converted_2012_d.pdf.

Extent of SBA Management and Technical Training Assistance, By Developmental Stage

As shown in **Table 1**, the survey indicated that SBDCs, WBCs, and SCORE served businesses at all three stages of development, with 44% of SBDC clients being either a nascent (25%) or startup (19%) client; 55% of SCORE clients being either a nascent (33%) or startup (22%) client; and 47% of WBC clients being either a nascent (32%) or startup (15%) client.

Table 1. SBA Management and Technical Assistance Training Programs' Clients, Percentage by Client Business Development Stage, 2011

SBA Resource Partner	Nascent	Startup	In-Business	Total
Small Business Development Centers	25%	19%	56%	100%
SCORE	33%	22%	45%	100%
Women Business Centers	32%	15%	53%	100%

Source: U.S. Small Business Administration, Office of Entrepreneurial Development, "Impact Study of Entrepreneurial Dynamics: Office of Entrepreneurial Development Resource Partners' Face-to-Face Counseling," September 2012, pp. 5, 9, at http://www.sba.gov/sites/default/files/files/SBA_Converted_2012_d.pdf.

Notes: The survey's authors defined nascent clients as individuals who have taken one or more steps to start a business; startup clients as individuals who have been in business one year or less; and in-business clients as individuals who have been in business more than one year and their business was classified as small by the SBA.

Impact of the SBA's Management and Technical Training Assistance, by Developmental Stage

The survey asked SBA management and training assistance participants if they thought that the information they received from counselors was extremely useful, useful, no opinion, somewhat useful, or not useful.

As shown in **Table 2**, most of the SBDC, WBC, and SCORE clients that responded to the survey, including both nascent and startup clients, rated the usefulness of the information provided during their face-to-face management and technical assistance training as either extremely useful or useful.

Table 2. Usefulness of SBA Management and Technical Assistance Training Programs, Percentage by Client Business Development Stage, 2011

(percentage responding extremely useful or useful)

SBA Resource Partner	Nascent	Startup	In-Business	Overall
Small Business Development Centers	81%	81%	76%	79%
SCORE	76%	72%	71%	73%
Women Business Centers	75%	84%	78%	79%

Source: U.S. Small Business Administration, Office of Entrepreneurial Development, "Impact Study of Entrepreneurial Dynamics: Office of Entrepreneurial Development Resource Partners' Face-to-Face Counseling," September 2012, pp. 38, 50, 62, at http://www.sba.gov/sites/default/files/files/SBA_Converted_2012_d.pdf.

Notes: The survey's authors defined nascent clients as individuals who have taken one or more steps to start a business; startup clients as individuals who have been in business one year or less; and in-business clients as individuals who have been in business more than one year and their business was classified as small by the SBA.

The survey also asked SBA management and training assistance participants if they had changed their management practices or strategies as a result of the SBA management and technical assistance training they received.

As shown in **Table 3**, more than half of SBDC and SCORE startup clients that responded to the survey reported that they had changed their management practices or strategies as a result of the SBA management and technical assistance training they received, slightly less than the percentages reported by in-business clients. In comparison, three-quarters of WBC startup clients that responded to the survey reported that they changed their management practices or strategies as a result of the assistance they received, somewhat higher than the percentage reported by in-business clients.

Table 3. Percentage of Businesses That Changed Their Management Practices/Strategies As a Result of the SBA Management and Technical Assistance Training Received, by Client Business Development Stage, 2011

(percentage responding yes)

SBA Resource Partner	Startup	In-Business
Small Business Development Centers	56%	60%
SCORE	57%	61%
Women Business Centers	75%	59%

Source: U.S. Small Business Administration, Office of Entrepreneurial Development, "Impact Study of Entrepreneurial Dynamics: Office of Entrepreneurial Development Resource Partners' Face-to-Face Counseling," September 2012, pp. 40, 52, 64, at http://www.sba.gov/sites/default/files/files/SBA_Converted_2012_d.pdf.

Notes: The survey's authors defined startup clients as individuals who have been in business one year or less; and in-business clients as individuals who have been in business more than one year and their business was classified as small by the SBA.

As shown in **Table 4**, 14% of SBDC startup clients, 11% of SCORE startup clients, and 12% of WBC startup clients that responded to the survey reported that they either agreed or strongly agreed with the statement that the SBA management and technical assistance training they received enabled them to retain current staff, somewhat less than the percentages reported by in-business clients.

Table 4. Percentage of Businesses That Retained Current Staff As a Result of the SBA Management and Training Technical Assistance Received, by Client Business Development Stage, 2011

(percentage responding agree or strongly agree)

SBA Resource Partner	Startup	In-Business
Small Business Development Centers	14%	26%
SCORE	11%	19%
Women Business Centers	12%	22%

Source: U.S. Small Business Administration, Office of Entrepreneurial Development, "Impact Study of Entrepreneurial Dynamics: Office of Entrepreneurial Development Resource Partners' Face-to-Face Counseling," September 2012, pp. 42, 54, 66, at http://www.sba.gov/sites/default/files/files/SBA_Converted_2012_d.pdf.

Notes: The survey's authors defined startup clients as individuals who have been in business one year or less; and in-business clients as individuals who have been in business more than one year and their business was classified as small by the SBA.

As shown in **Table 5**, 13% of SBDC startup clients, 10% of SCORE startup clients, and 10% of WBC startup clients that responded to the survey reported that they either agreed or strongly agreed with the statement that the SBA management and technical assistance training they received enabled them to hire new staff, somewhat less than the percentages reported by in-business clients.

Table 5. Percentage of Businesses That Hired New Staff As a Result of the SBA Management and Training Technical Assistance Received, by Client Business Development Stage, 2011

(percentage responding agree or strongly agree)

SBA Resource Partner	Startup	In-Business
Small Business Development Centers	13%	20%
SCORE	10%	16%
Women Business Centers	10%	15%

Source: U.S. Small Business Administration, Office of Entrepreneurial Development, "Impact Study of Entrepreneurial Dynamics: Office of Entrepreneurial Development Resource Partners' Face-to-Face Counseling," September 2012, pp. 42, 54, 66, at http://www.sba.gov/sites/default/files/files/SBA_Converted_2012_d.pdf.

Notes: The survey's authors defined startup clients as individuals who have been in business one year or less; and in-business clients as individuals who have been in business more than one year and their business was classified as small by the SBA.

As shown in **Table 6**, 30% of SBDC startup clients, 24% of SCORE startup clients, and 31% of WBC startup clients that responded to the survey reported that they either agreed or strongly agreed with the statement that the SBA management and technical assistance training they received had a positive impact on their profit margin, somewhat less than the percentages reported by in-business clients.

Table 6. Percentage of Businesses That Experienced an Increase in Their Profit Margin As a Result of the SBA Management and Training Technical Assistance Received, by Client Business Development Stage, 2011

(percentage responding agree or strongly agree)

SBA Resource Partner	Startup	In-Business
Small Business Development Centers	30%	32%
SCORE	24%	28%
Women Business Centers	31%	34%

Source: U.S. Small Business Administration, Office of Entrepreneurial Development, "Impact Study of Entrepreneurial Dynamics: Office of Entrepreneurial Development Resource Partners' Face-to-Face Counseling," September 2012, pp. 42, 54, 66, at http://www.sba.gov/sites/default/files/files/SBA_Converted_2012_d.pdf.

Notes: The survey's authors defined startup clients as individuals who have been in business one year or less; and in-business clients as individuals who have been in business more than one year and their business was classified as small by the SBA.

The SBA's Growth Accelerators Initiative

Growth accelerators are organizations that help entrepreneurs start and scale their business. Accelerators are typically run by experienced entrepreneurs and help small businesses, especially startups, "access seed capital, mentors, and networking opportunities for customers and partners" and provide "targeted advice on revenue growth, employee growth, sourcing outside funding and avoiding pitfalls."[30] In 2012, the SBA hosted four regional events (Northeast, Midwest, South, and Mid-Atlantic), which were attended by representatives "from over 100 universities and accelerators to discuss working with high-growth entrepreneurs."[31] These meetings "culminated in a White House event co-hosted by the SBA and the Department of Commerce which will help formalize the network of universities and accelerators, provide a series of "train the trainer" events on various government programs that benefit high-growth entrepreneurs, and provide a playbook of best practices on engaging universities on innovation and entrepreneurship."[32]

The Obama Administration requested $5 million in its FY2014 budget request to expand the SBA's growth accelerators initiative.[33] The Administration indicated that it wanted to spend $5 million per year for five years to support university and private-sector growth accelerators by awarding them competitive grants, awarded on a 4:1 matching ratio of private to public funding. Organizations selected for funding would build upon the lessons learned during 2012 meetings and "scale what already works best" and have a proven record of success.[34]

In its "Explanatory Statement" accompanying the Consolidated Appropriations Act, 2014, Congress recommended that the SBA's growth accelerators initiative receive $2.5 million in FY2014.[35] Although there was no public debate concerning the funding level to be provided the initiative, opposition to providing additional funding for the growth accelerators initiative most likely focused on concerns about duplication of management and training efforts, both within the SBA and among federal agencies; the SBA's use of initiatives in the absence of explicit congressional approval; and budgetary impact.[36]

---

[30] U.S. Small Business Administration, "FY2014 Congressional Budget Justification and FY2012 Annual Performance Report," p. 59, at http://www.sba.gov/sites/default/files/files/1-FY%202014%20CBJ%20FY%202012%20APR.PDF.

[31] Ibid.

[32] Ibid., pp. 59-60.

[33] Ibid., p. 60.

[34] U.S. Small Business Administration, "FY2014 Congressional Budget Justification and FY2012 Annual Performance Report," p. 60, at http://www.sba.gov/sites/default/files/files/1-FY%202014%20CBJ%20FY%202012%20APR.PDF.

[35] Recommended funding levels for the SBA's noncredit programs are provided in the "Explanatory Statement" accompanying the Consolidated Appropriations Act, 2014 (Division E- Financial Services and General Government Appropriations Act, 2014), pp. 37-39, at http://docs.house.gov/billsthisweek/20140113/113-HR3547-JSOM-D-F.pdf. Although not legally binding, the SBA has traditionally adhered to the recommended funding levels for noncredit programs contained in the report or statement accompanying the annual appropriations act funding the agency.

[36] See U.S. Congress, House Committee on Small Business, "Views and Estimates of the Committee on Small Business on Matters to be set forth in the Concurrent Resolution on the Budget for FY2014," communication to the Chairman, House Committee on the Budget, 113th Cong., 1st sess., February 27, 2013, at http://smallbusiness.house.gov/uploadedfiles/revised_2014_views_and_estimates_document.pdf; and Barry Pineles, Chief Counsel, House Committee on Small Business, "Hearing Memorandum on The Budget Outlook for Small Business Administration, April 18, (continued...)

SBA Lending Programs

The SBA's business lending programs are designed to encourage lenders to provide loans to small businesses "that might not otherwise obtain financing on reasonable terms and conditions."[37] Historically, the SBA's lending programs have been justified on the grounds that small businesses can be at a disadvantage, compared with other businesses, when trying to obtain access to sufficient capital and credit.[38] As an economist explained,

> Growing firms need resources, but many small firms may have a hard time obtaining loans because they are young and have little credit history. Lenders may also be reluctant to lend to small firms with innovative products because it might be difficult to collect enough reliable information to correctly estimate the risk for such products. If it's true that the lending process leaves worthy projects unfunded, some suggest that it would be good to fix this "market failure" with government programs aimed at improving small businesses' access to credit.[39]

In FY2013, the SBA enhanced small business access to capital by guaranteeing more than $18.7 billion in loans to small businesses. The SBA's two largest loan guaranty programs are the 7(a) loan guaranty program ($14.7 billion disbursed in FY2013) and the 504/CDC loan guaranty program ($4.0 billion disbursed in FY2013). In addition, the SBA's Microloan program, which includes startups among its targeted audiences, provides direct loans to 180 qualified non-profit intermediary Microloan lenders to provide "microloans" of up to $50,000 to small business owners, entrepreneurs, and non-profit child care centers. The Microloan program provided $51.2 million in loans to small businesses in FY2013.[40]

The SBA's 7(a), 504/CDC, and Microloan Programs

7(a) Loan Guaranty Program[41]

The SBA's 7(a) loan guaranty program is considered the agency's flagship loan guaranty program.[42] It is named from Section 7(a) of the Small Business Act of 1953 (P.L. 83-163, as

---

(...continued)

2013," p. 26, at http://smallbusiness house.gov/uploadedfiles/revised_hearing_memo_4-24-2013.pdf.

[37] U.S. Small Business Administration, *Fiscal Year 2010 Congressional Budget Justification*, p. 30.

[38] Proponents of providing federal funding for the SBA's loan guarantee programs also argue that small business can promote competitive markets. See P.L. 83-163, §2(a), as amended; and 15 U.S.C. §631a.

[39] Veronique de Rugy, *Why the Small Business Administration's Loan Programs Should Be Abolished*, American Enterprise Institute for Public Policy Research, AEI Working Paper #126, April 13, 2006, at http://www.aei.org/files/2006/04/13/20060414_wp126.pdf. Also, see U.S. Government Accountability Office, *Small Business Administration: 7(a) Loan Program Needs Additional Performance Measures*, GAO-08-226T, November 1, 2007, pp. 3, 9-11, at http://www.gao.gov/new.items/d08226t.pdf.

[40] U.S Small Business Administration, "Microloan Nationwide Loan Report, October 1, 2012 through September 30, 2013," October 28, 2013.

[41] For further information and analysis concerning the SBA's 7(a) program see CRS Report R41146, *Small Business Administration 7(a) Loan Guaranty Program*, by Robert Jay Dilger.

[42] U.S. Congress, House Committee on Small Business, Subcommittee on Finance and Tax, *Subcommittee Hearing on Improving the SBA's Access to Capital Programs for Our Nation's Small Business*, 110th Cong., 2nd sess., March 5, 2008, H.Hrg. 110-76 (Washington: GPO, 2008), p. 2.

---

amended), which authorizes the SBA to provide business loans to American small businesses. The SBA provides participating, certified lenders a guaranty of repayment in the case of a default of up to 85% of qualified loan amounts of $150,000 or less and up to 75% of qualified loan amounts exceeding $150,000 to the program's loan limit of $5 million.

Proceeds from 7(a) loans may be used to establish a new business or to assist in the operation, acquisition, or expansion of an existing business. Specific uses include to acquire land (by purchase or lease); improve a site (e.g., grading, streets, parking lots, and landscaping); purchase, convert, expand, or renovate one or more existing buildings; construct one or more new buildings; acquire (by purchase or lease) and install fixed assets; purchase inventory, supplies, and raw materials; finance working capital; and refinance certain outstanding debts.[43]

504 Certified Development Company Loan Guaranty Program[44]

The SBA's 504 Certified Development Company (504/CDC) loan guaranty program provides long-term fixed rate financing for major fixed assets, such as land, buildings, equipment, and machinery. A 504/CDC loan cannot be used for working capital or inventory. It is named from Section 504 of the Small Business Investment Act of 1958 (P.L. 85-699, as amended), which authorized the sale of debentures pursuant to Section 503 of the act, which previously authorized the program.[45]

The 504/CDC program is administered through non-profit CDCs. Of the total project costs, a third-party lender must provide at least 50% of the financing, the CDC provides up to 40% of the financing backed by a 100% SBA-guaranteed debenture, and the applicant provides at least 10% of the financing.

The SBA's debenture is backed with the full faith and credit of the United States and is sold to underwriters who form debenture pools. Investors purchase interests in the debenture pools and receive certificates representing ownership of all or part of the pool. The SBA and CDCs use various agents to facilitate the sale and service of the certificates and the orderly flow of funds among the parties.[46] After a 504/CDC loan is approved and disbursed, accounting for the loan is set up at the Central Servicing Agent (CSA, currently Colson Services Corporation), not the SBA. The SBA guarantees the timely payment of the debenture. If the small business is behind in its loan payments, the SBA pays the difference to the investor on every semi-annual due date.[47]

---

[43] 13 C.F.R. §120.120.

[44] For further information and analysis of the SBA's 504/CDC program see CRS Report R41184, *Small Business Administration 504/CDC Loan Guaranty Program*, by Robert Jay Dilger.

[45] The 504/CDC program was preceded by a 501 state development company program (1958-1982), a 502 local development company program (1958-1995), and a 503/CDC program (1980-1986). The 504/CDC program started in 1986. There are a small number of for-profit CDCs that participated in these predecessor programs that have been grandfathered into the current 504/CDC program. See U.S. Small Business Administration, "SOP 50 10 5(F): Lender and Development Company Loan Programs," (effective January 1, 2014), p. 44, at http://www.sba.gov/sites/default/files/Clean%20FINAL%20SOP%2050%2010%205%20(F).pdf.

[46] 13 C.F.R. §120.801. 504/CDC debentures are normally sold and proceeds disbursed on the Wednesday after the second Sunday of each month. See U.S. Small Business Administration, "SOP 50 10 5(F): Lender and Development Company Loan Programs," (effective January 1, 2014), p. 319, at http://www.sba.gov/sites/default/files/Clean%20FINAL%20SOP%2050%2010%205%20(F).pdf.

[47] U.S. Small Business Administration, "Monthly Purchase of 504 Debentures for Accelerated Loans," at http://archive.sba.gov/aboutsba/sbaprograms/elending/notices/BANK_5000_602_MONTHLY_PURC_504.html.

The 504/CDC program is somewhat unique in that borrowers must meet one of two specified economic development objectives. First, borrowers, other than small manufacturers, must create or retain at least one job for every $65,000 of project debenture. Borrowers who are small manufacturers must create or retain one job per $100,000 of project debenture. The jobs created do not have to be at the project facility, but 75% of the jobs must be created in the community where the project is located. Using job retention to satisfy this requirement is allowed only if the CDC "can reasonably show that jobs would be lost to the community if the project was not done."[48]

Second, if the borrower does not meet the job creation or retention requirement, the borrower can retain eligibility by meeting any one of five community development goals or ten public policy goals, provided the CDC meets its required job opportunity average of at least one job opportunity created or retained for every $65,000 in project debenture, or for every $75,000 in project debenture for projects located in special geographic areas (Alaska, Hawaii, state-designated enterprise zones, empowerment zones, enterprise communities, and labor surplus areas). Loans to small manufacturers are excluded from the calculation of this average.[49]

The Microloan Program[50]

The SBA's Microloan program was authorized in 1991 (P.L. 102-140, the Departments of Commerce, Justice, and State, the Judiciary, and Related Agencies Appropriations Act, 1992) as a five-year demonstration program to address the perceived disadvantages faced by very small businesses in gaining access to capital. The program became operational in 1992, and it was made permanent, subject to reauthorization, in 1997 (P.L. 105-135, the Small Business Reauthorization Act of 1997). Its stated purpose is

> to assist women, low-income, veteran ... and minority entrepreneurs and business owners and other individuals possessing the capability to operate successful business concerns; to assist small business concerns in those areas suffering from a lack of credit due to economic downturns; ... to make loans to eligible intermediaries to enable such intermediaries to provide small-scale loans, particularly loans in amounts averaging not more than $10,000, to start-up, newly established, or growing small business concerns for working capital or the acquisition of materials, supplies, or equipment; [and] to make grants to eligible intermediaries that, together with non-Federal matching funds, will enable such intermediaries to provide intensive marketing, management, and technical assistance to microloan borrowers.[51]

The maximum Microloan amount is $50,000 and no borrower may owe an intermediary more than $50,000 at any one time.[52] Microloan proceeds may be used only for working capital and

---

[48] U.S. Small Business Administration, "SOP 50 10 5(F): Lender and Development Company Loan Programs," (effective January 1, 2014), p. 276, at http://www.sba.gov/sites/default/files/Clean%20FINAL%20SOP%2050%2010%205%20(F).pdf.

[49] A job opportunity is defined as a full time (or equivalent) permanent job created within two years of receipt of 504/CDC funds, or retained in the community because of a 504/CDC loan. See ibid., pp. 51, 237, 276.

[50] For further information and analysis concerning the SBA's Microloan program, see CRS Report R41057, *Small Business Administration Microloan Program*, by Robert Jay Dilger.

[51] 15 U.S.C. §636 7(m)(1)(A).

[52] 13 C.F.R §120.707. P.L. 111-240, the Small Business Jobs Act of 2010, increased the loan limit for borrowers from $35,000 to $50,000.

---

acquisition of materials, supplies, furniture, fixtures, and equipment. Loans cannot be made to acquire land or property, and must be repaid within six years.[53] Within these parameters, loan terms vary depending on the loan's size, the planned use of funds, the requirements of the intermediary lender, and the needs of the small business borrower. Interest rates are negotiated between the borrower and the intermediary (within statutory limits), and typically range from 8% to 10%.[54] Each intermediary establishes its own lending and credit requirements. However, borrowers are generally required to provide some type of collateral, and a personal guarantee to repay the loan. The SBA does not review the loan for creditworthiness.[55]

Program Performance

The SBA maintains a relatively extensive output database for its business lending programs (e.g., number and amount of loans approved and disbursed by program and by year; number and amount of loans approved and disbursed by program and by year to various demographic groups, including startups; number and amount of loans approved and disbursed by program by state; amount of loan purchases and recoveries by program and by year). It also asks borrowers to report information concerning the impact the loans have on job creation and retention.

As will be shown, these data suggest that the SBA provides lending support to small businesses at all stages of development, but to varying degrees, with the Microloan program providing a relatively higher share of its lending to startups than the 7(a) and 504/CDC programs. The data also suggest that these programs have a generally positive impact on job creation and retention, but, as will be discussed, the data are self-reported and subject to methodological limitations.

Extent of SBA Lending Assistance, By Developmental Stage

As shown in **Table 7**, from FY2011 through FY2013, as expected given their missions, the Microloan program issued, as a percentage of total disbursements, more loans to startups (ranging from 35.9% to 40.7% of total disbursements) than the 7(a) program (ranging from 22.1% to 26.4% of total disbursements) and the 504/CDC program (ranging from 10.0% to 13.3% of total disbursements).

Table 7. 7(a), 504/CDC and Microloan Disbursements, by Development Stage, FY2011-FY2013

Development Stage	FY2011	FY2012	FY2013
7(a) Startup	$3,609,994,440 (22.1%)	$3,720,402,691 (26.4%)	$3,950,334,034 (26.3%)
7(a) In-Business	$12,656,161,854 (77.4%)	$10,333,125,711 (73.5%)	$11,044,549,765 (73.6%)

---

[53] Ibid.

[54] In FY2012, Microloan borrowers were charged, on average, an interest rate of 8.18, compared with 8.45% in FY2011. U.S Small Business Administration, "Microloan Nationwide Loan Report, October 1, 2011 through September 30, 2012," October 15, 2012; and U.S Small Business Administration, "Microloan Nationwide Loan Report, October 1, 2010 through September 30, 2011," November 2, 2011.

[55] U.S. Small Business Administration, "Microloan Program," at http://www.sba.gov/content/microloan-program.

Development Stage	FY2011	FY2012	FY2013
7(a) unknown	$75,519,608 (0.5%)	$11,781,996 (0.1%)	$15,872,030 (0.1%)
Total 7(a)	$16,341,675,902 (100.0%)	$14,065,310,398 (100.0%)	$15,016,144,072 (100.0%)
504/CDC Startup	$484,060,000 (13.3%)	$490,687,000 (10.5%)	$509,053,000 (10.0%)
504/CDC In-Business	$3,166,821,000 (86.7%)	$4,198,411,000 (89.5%)	$4,570,902,000 (90.0%)
504/CDC Total	$3,650,881,000 (100.0%)	$4,689,098,000 (100.0%)	$5,079,955,000 (100.0%)
Microloan Startup	$16,811,279 (35.9%)	$16,766,240 (37.5%)	$20,851,860 (40.7%)
Microloan In-Business	$30,006,149 (64.1%)	$27,947,887 (62.5%)	$30,352,085 (59.2%)
Microloan Total	$46,817,428 (100.0%)	$44,714,127 (100.0%)	$51,203,945 (100.0%)

Source: U.S. Small Business Administration, "Microloan Nationwide Loan Report," various fiscal years; and U.S. Small Business Administration, Office of Congressional and Legislative Affairs, February 18, 2014.

Notes: Startup borrowers are individuals who have been in business one year or less. In-business borrowers are individuals who have been in business more than one year and their business was classified as small by the SBA.

Impact of the SBA's Lending Assistance on Job Creation and Retention, by Developmental Stage

Unlike its management and technical assistance training programs, the SBA does not survey SBA loan recipients after the loans are issued to determine the loan's impact on the borrowers' staffing decisions or on the business's subsequent economic activities (sales, profits, etc.).

However, 7(a) loan guaranty program application forms require borrowers to include information concerning the number of employees at the time of application and the number of jobs to be created or retained as a result of the loan. Jobs "created" means the number of full-time (or equivalent) employees that the small business expects to hire as a result of the loan. Jobs "retained" means the number of full-time (or equivalent) employees on the payroll of the business at the time of application that will be lost if the loan is not approved.[56] Lenders transmit the data to the SBA. Largely because the data are not verified by the SBA, the SBA refers to these data as the number of jobs supported, as opposed to the number of jobs created and retained.

In the 504/CDC loan guaranty program, where job creation and retention is a program criterion, applicants are required to report the number of current employees, jobs to be created in the next two years, and jobs to be retained because of the loan. CDCs must list the estimated jobs created

---

[56] U.S. Small Business Administration, "SOP 50 10 5(F): Lender and Development Company Loan Programs," (effective January 1, 2014), p. 196, at http://www.sba.gov/sites/default/files/ Clean%20FINAL%20SOP%2050%2010%205%20(F).pdf; and U.S. Small Business Administration, Office of the Inspector General, "Review of SBA's Job Creation Data Under the Recovery Act," p. 2, at http://www.sba.gov/sites/ default/files/oig_report_10-15.pdf.

or retained in its annual report to the SBA, and at the two-year anniversary of each loan's disbursement CDCs must list the actual number of full-time equivalent jobs created or retained for that loan (whether the initial approval was based on job creation/retention or some other 504 goal).[57] Again, for methodological reasons, the SBA refers to this data as the number of jobs supported, as opposed to the number of jobs created and retained.

Each time a Microloan is made, the SBA requires that the loan either create or retain at least one job. Beyond that job, the Microloan intermediary must also account for any other jobs created or retained (counted in terms of full time equivalents) and report that data to the SBA. The SBA reserves the right to verify the correctness of the number of jobs created or retained during any visit to a Microloan intermediary or a Microloan borrower's site. The SBA reports the data as the number of jobs supported.[58]

As shown in **Table 8**, from FY2011 through FY2013, the Microloan program provided startups a higher proportion of the total number of jobs it supported than either the 7(a) or the 504/CDC programs. This finding might have been expected, given that startups are one of the Microloan program's primary target audiences.

As shown in the table, from FY2011 to FY2013, startups accounted for 49.4% to 55.9% of the total number of jobs supported in the Microloan program, for 23.2% to 26.8% of the total number of jobs supported in the 7(a) program, and for 11.6% to 14.6% of the total number of jobs supported in the 504/CDC program.

---

[57] U.S. Small Business Administration, "SOP 50 10 5(F): Lender and Development Company Loan Programs," (effective January 1, 2014), p. 276, at http://www.sba.gov/sites/default/files/ Clean%20FINAL%20SOP%2050%2010%205%20(F).pdf; and U.S. Small Business Administration, Office of the Inspector General, "Review of SBA's Job Creation Data Under the Recovery Act," p. 2, at http://www.sba.gov/sites/ default/files/oig_report_10-15.pdf.

[58] U.S. Small Business Administration, "SOP 52 00: Microloan Program," p. 56, at http://www.sba.gov/sites/default/ files/Microloan%20SOP%2052%2000%20(FINAL).pdf.

Table 8. 7(a), 504/CDC and Microloan Programs, Reported Number of Jobs Supported by Development Stage, FY2011-FY2013

Development Stage	FY2011	FY2012	FY2013
7(a) Startup	134,991 (23.2%)	119,029 (26.2%)	129,637 (26.8%)
7(a) In-Business	447,716 (76.8%)	335,785 (73.8%)	354,339 (73.2%)
Total 7(a)	582,707 (100.0%)	454,814 (100.0%)	483,976 (100.0%)
504/CDC Startup	12,742 (14.6%)	13,549 (11.6%)	13,205 (14.6%)
504/CDC In-Business	74,595 (85.4%)	103,020 (88.4%)	77,052 (85.4%)
504/CDC Total	87,337 (100.0%)	116,569 (100.0%)	90,257 (100.0%)
Microloan Startup	6,555 (49.4%)	6,685 (50.3%)	8,741 (55.9%)
Microloan In-Business	6,716 (50.6%)	6,595 (49.7%)	6,895 (44.1%)
Microloan Total	13,271 (100.0%)	13,280 (100.0%)	15,636 (100.0%)

Source: U.S. Small Business Administration, Office of Congressional and Legislative Affairs, April 8, 2013; and U.S. Small Business Administration, Office of Congressional and Legislative Affairs, February 25, 2014.

Notes: Startup borrowers are individuals who have been in business one year or less. In-business borrowers are individuals who have been in business more than one year and their business was classified as small by the SBA.

SBA Venture Capital Programs

The SBA has two venture capital programs. The SBIC program, authorized by P.L. 85-699, the Small Business Investment Act of 1958, as amended, is the SBA's flagship venture capital program.[59] It is designed to "improve and stimulate the national economy in general and the small business segment thereof in particular" by stimulating and supplementing "the flow of private equity capital and long-term loan funds which small business concerns need for the sound financing of their business operations and for their growth, expansion, and modernization, and which are not available in adequate supply."[60] The SBA also sponsors the much smaller New Markets Venture Capital Program, which is not discussed here given its relatively small size ($1,464,802 in financing to 10 small businesses in FY2013). It is designed to promote economic development and the creation of wealth and job opportunities in low-income geographic areas by addressing the unmet equity investments needs of small businesses located in those areas.[61]

---

[59] For further information and analysis of the SBA's SBIC program see CRS Report R41456, *SBA Small Business Investment Company Program*, by Robert Jay Dilger.

[60] 15 U.S.C. §661.

[61] For further information and analysis of the SBA's New Markets Venture Capital program see CRS Report R42565, *SBA New Markets Venture Capital Program*, by Robert Jay Dilger.

The SBIC Program

The SBA does not make direct investments in small businesses. It partners with privately owned and managed SBICs licensed by the SBA to provide financing to small businesses with private capital the SBIC has raised (called regulatory capital) and with funds (called leverage) the SBIC borrows at favorable rates because the SBA guarantees the debenture (loan obligation). As of December 31, 2013, there were 287 licensed SBICs participating in the SBIC program.[62]

A licensed debenture SBIC in good standing, with a demonstrated need for funds, may apply to the SBA for financial assistance (leverage) of up to 300% of its private capital. However, the SBA has traditionally approved debenture SBICs for a maximum of 200% of their private capital and no fund management team may exceed the allowable maximum amount of leverage of $150 million per SBIC and $225 million for two or more licenses under common control.[63] A SBIC licensed on or after October 1, 2009, may elect to have a maximum leverage amount of $175 million per SBIC and $250 million for two or more licenses under common control if it has invested at least 50% of its financings in low-income geographic areas and certifies that at least 50% of its future investments will be in low-income geographic areas.[64]

SBICs pursue investments in a broad range of industries, geographic areas, and stages of investment. Some SBICs specialize in a particular field or industry, while others invest more generally. Most SBICs concentrate on a particular stage of investment (i.e., startup, expansion, or turnaround) and geographic area.

SBICs provide equity capital to small businesses in various ways, including by

- purchasing small business equity securities (e.g., stock, stock options, warrants, limited partnership interests, membership interests in a limited liability company, or joint venture interests);[65]

- making loans to small businesses, either independently or in cooperation with other private or public lenders, that have a maturity of no more than 20 years;[66]

---

[62] U.S. Small Business Administration, "SBIC Program Overview, as of December 31, 2013," at http://www.sba.gov/content/quarterly-sbic-program-statistics-0.

[63] 13 CFR §107.1120; 13 CFR §107.1150; and U.S. Small Business Administration, "American Recovery and Reinvestment Act of 2009: Implementation of SBIC Program Changes," letter from Harry Haskins, Acting Associate Administrator for Investment, to All Small Business Investment Companies (SBICs) and Applicants, May 4, 2009, p. 1, at http://archive.sba.gov/idc/groups/public/documents/sba_program_office/inv_rcvry_act_sbic_changes.pdf.

[64] 13 CFR §107.1150. A low-income area is (1) any population census tract that has a poverty rate that is not less than 20% or (a) if located within a metropolitan area, 50% or more of the households in that census tract have an income equal to less than 60% of the area median gross income; or (b) if not located within a metropolitan area, the median household income in that census tract does not exceed 80% of the statewide median household income; or (c) has been determined by the SBA Administrator to contain a substantial population of low-income individuals in residence, an inadequate access to investment capital, or other indications of economic distress; or (2) any area located within (i) a Historically Underutilized Business Zone; (ii) an Urban Empowerment Zone or Urban Enterprise Community (as designated by the Secretary of the United States Department of Housing and Urban Development); or (iii) a Rural Empowerment Zone or Rural Enterprise Community (as designated by the Secretary of the United States Department of Agriculture). See 13 CFR §108.50.

[65] 13 CFR §107.800. A SBIC is not allowed to become a general partner in any unincorporated business or become jointly or severally liable for any obligations of an unincorporated business.

[66] 13 CFR §107.810; and 13 CFR §107.840.

- purchasing debt securities from small businesses;[67] and

- providing small businesses (subject to limitations) a guarantee of their monetary obligations to creditors not associated with the SBIC.[68]

The SBA is authorized to provide up to $4 billion in leverage to SBICs annually. The SBIC program has invested or committed about $19.9 billion in small businesses, with the SBA's share of capital at risk about $9.5 billion. In FY2013, the SBA committed to guarantee $2.15 billion in SBIC small business investments, and SBICs invested another $1.34 billion from private capital, for almost $3.5 billion in financing for 1,068 small businesses.[69]

Early Stage Debenture SBICs

On April 27, 2012, the SBA published a final rule in the Federal Register establishing a $1 billion early stage debenture SBIC initiative (up to $150 million in leverage in FY2012, and up to $200 million in leverage per fiscal year thereafter until the limit is reached).[70] Early stage debenture SBICs are required to invest at least 50% of their financings in early stage small businesses, defined as small businesses that have never achieved positive cash flow from operations in any fiscal year.[71]

In recognition of the higher risk associated with investments in early stage small businesses, the initiative includes "several new regulatory provisions intended to reduce the risk that an early stage SBIC would default on its leverage and to improve SBA's recovery prospects should a default occur."[72] For example, early stage debenture SBICs are required to raise more regulatory capital (at least $20 million) than debenture SBICs (at least $5 million). They are also subject to special distribution rules to require pro rata repayment of SBA leverage when making distributions of profits to their investors. In addition, early stage debenture SBICs are also provided less leverage (up to 100% of regulatory capital, $50 million maximum) than debenture SBICs (up to 200% of regulatory capital, $150 million maximum per SBIC and $225 million for two or more SBICs under common control).

On May 1, 2012, the SBA published a notice in the *Federal Register* inviting venture capital fund managers to submit an application to become a licensed early stage debenture SBIC. The application deadline for applicants with signed commitments for at least $15 million in regulatory capital and evidence of their ability to raise the remaining $5 million in regulatory capital was set as July 30, 2012. The application deadline for all other applicants was set as May 15, 2013.[73] Thirty-three venture capital funds submitted preliminary application materials to participate in the

---

[67] 13 CFR §107.815. Debt securities are instruments evidencing a loan with an option or any other right to acquire equity securities in a small business or its affiliates, or a loan which by its terms is convertible into an equity position, or a loan with a right to receive royalties that are excluded from the cost of money.

[68] 13 CFR §107.820.

[69] U.S. Small Business Administration, "SBIC Program Overview, as of December 31, 2013," at http://www.sba.gov/content/quarterly-sbic-program-statistics-0.

[70] U.S. Small Business Administration, "Small Business Investment Companies - Early Stage SBICs," 77 *Federal Register* 25043, 25050, April 27, 2012.

[71] Ibid., pp. 25051-25053.

[72] Ibid., p. 25043.

[73] U.S. Small Business Administration, "Small Business Investment Companies - Early Stage SBICs," 77 *Federal Register* 25775-25779, May 1, 2012.

program. After these materials were examined and interviews held, the SBA announced on October 23, 2012, that it had issued "green light" letters to six funds, formally inviting these funds to file a license application.[74]

On December 18, 2012, the SBA published a notice in the *Federal Register* announcing its second annual call for venture capital fund managers to submit an application to become a licensed early stage debenture SBIC. The deadline for completing the four-step application process for applicants with signed commitments for at least $15 million in regulatory capital and evidence of their ability to raise the remaining $5 million in regulatory capital was set as June 7, 2013. The deadline for completing the four-step application process for all other applicants was set as September 27, 2013.[75]

As of October 31, 2013, three early stage SBICs had raised $133.9 million in private capital, received $4 million in leverage from the SBA, and invested $9.3 million in five small businesses.[76]

On February 4, 2014, the SBA issued its FY2014 call for venture capital fund managers to submit an application to become a licensed early stage debenture SBIC. The deadline for funds seeking a license in FY2014 was set as June 30, 2014, with an anticipated licensing date for FY2014 funds being no later than September 30, 2014.[77]

Program Performance

The SBA gathers a relatively robust list of SBIC program output measures, such as the number and amount of financing made each fiscal year, the number of active SBIC debenture firms, the use of proceeds (operating capital, plant modernization, acquisition of existing business, land acquisition, etc.), the type of financing provided (straight debt, debt with equity and equity only), licensing times, and financing by: industrial sector, type of small business (corporations, partnerships, proprietorships or limited liability corporations), state, region, demographic group, age of the licensee and, of particular interest here, age of the business at the time of the financing. The SBA does not gather information concerning the number of jobs supported by the program.

Extent of SBIC Financial Assistance, By Developmental Stage

The SBIC program provides financing to small businesses at all developmental stages, with most of its financing provided to businesses that have been in operation for at least five years. For example, in FY2013, 65.4% of the SBIC program's financing was with businesses that were in operation for at least five years ($2.287 billion of $3.498 billion). As shown in **Table 9**, the

---

[74] U.S. Small Business Administration, "SBA's Growth Capital Program Sets Record For Third Year in a Row $2.95 Billion in Financing for Small Businesses in FY12," at http://www.sba.gov/about-sba-services/7367/342171; and U.S. Small Business Administration, "The Small Business Investment Company (SBIC) Program: Annual Report FY2012," p. 20, at http://www.sba.gov/sites/default/files/files/SBIC%20Program%20FY%202012%20Annual%20Report.pdf.

[75] U.S. Small Business Administration, "Small Business Investment Companies - Early Stage SBICs," 77 *Federal Register* 74908-74913, December 18, 2012.

[76] U.S. Small Business Administration, Office of Congressional and Legislative Affairs, "Correspondence with the author," November 18, 2013.

[77] U.S. Small Business Administration, "Small Business Investment Companies—Early Stage SBICs," 79 *Federal Register* 6664-6668, February 4, 2014.

---

amount of SBIC financing provided to startups (defined as being in operation for one year or less) as a share of SBIC financing has increased somewhat since FY2011 (14.3% in FY2011, 16.8% in FY2012, and 19.9% in FY2013). The amount of SBIC financing to startups has also increased in recent years ($404.7 million in FY2011, $541.2 million in FY2012, and $696.7 million in FY2013).

It is too early to determine the extent to which the SBA's early stage debenture initiative may affect the share and amount of total SBA financing provided to startups.

Table 9. SBIC Program, Number and Amount of Financings by Development Stage, FY2011-FY2013

($ in thousands)

Development Stage	FY2011		FY2012		FY2013	
	#	Amount	#	Amount	#	Amount
Startup (1 year or less)	265 (11.7%)	$404,664 (14.3%)	224 (11.7%)	$541,189 (16.8%)	281 (15.2%)	$696,749 (19.9%)
In-Business (over 1 year)	2,005 (88.3%)	$2,428,706 (85.7%)	1,683 (88.3%)	$2,686,241 (83.2%)	1,565 (84.8%)	$2,801,565 (80.1%)
Total SBIC Financings	2,270 (100.0%)	$2,833,371 (100.0%)	1,907 (100.0%)	$3,227,430 (100.0%)	1,846 (100.0%)	$3,498,314 (100.0%)

Source: U.S. Small Business Administration, "All SBIC Program Licensees: Financing to Small Businesses," various fiscal years.

Concluding Observations

The SBA has indicated, from the very start of the agency, that assisting small businesses create and retain jobs is part of its mission. However, the SBA also has a long-established tradition of providing assistance to all qualifying small businesses. With some exceptions, the SBA has generally not taken actions or requested authorization to focus its assistance solely onto those businesses, such as startups, that are judged to be the ones most likely to contribute to job growth or wealth creation. The tradition of providing SBA assistance to all qualified small businesses without regard to their potential for job growth or wealth creation is perhaps understandable given that the tradition aligns with one of the SBA's primary missions, which is to promote free markets—by limiting monopoly and oligarchy formation within all industries. In addition, the tradition of providing assistance to all qualified small businesses has, for the most part, never been challenged by Congress or interested small business organizations.

The SBA's recent initiatives to focus increased attention to assisting startups (e.g., the Growth Accelerators initiative and the Early Stage Debenture SBIC initiative) are less of a challenge to the SBA's tradition of assisting all qualified small businesses than a recognition of the potential role of startups in job creation and concerns about the pace of job growth during the current economic recovery. For example, the SBA has offered the initiatives as supplements to, rather than replacements of, existing programs. Moreover, as has been discussed, the SBA's recent effort to enhance the ability of startups to access venture capital through the SBIC program is not without precedent within the agency. Although the SBA has not explicitly indicated that the Early Stage Debenture SBIC initiative is designed to fill the void left by the winding down of the SBIC

Participating Securities program, the SBA has acknowledged the lessons learned from that program in the development of regulations to manage risk within the Early Stage Debenture SBIC initiative.[78]

As mentioned previously, the relatively "high risk-high reward" of targeting SBA assistance to startups makes it tempting for some and controversial for others. Most who have participated in these programs report in surveys sponsored by the SBA that the programs were useful. However, determining if the risk of financial losses associated with targeting SBA assistance to startups outweighs the startups' potential for job growth is difficult because the data collected by the SBA concerning these programs' impact on economic activity and job creation are somewhat limited and subject to methodological challenges concerning their validity as reliable performance measures.

Author Contact Information

Robert Jay Dilger
Senior Specialist in American National Government
rdilger@crs.loc.gov, 7-3110

---

[78] U.S. Small Business Administration, "Small Business Investment Companies - Early Stage SBICs," 76 *Federal Register* 76907-76917, December 9, 2011; and U.S. Small Business Administration, "Small Business Investment Companies - Early Stage SBICs," 77 *Federal Register* 25042-25055, April 27, 2012.